Cornerstones of Freedom

The Library of Congress

GAIL SAKURAI

CHILDREN'S PRESS®
A Division of Grolier Publishing
New York • London • Hong Kong • Sydney
Danbury, Connecticut

Visit Children's Press on the Internet at:
http://publishing.grolier.com

Library of Congress Cataloging-in-Publication Data

Sakurai, Gail.
   The Library of Congress / by Gail Sakurai.
      p. cm.— (Cornerstones of freedom)
   Includes index.
   Summary: Describes the history of the Library of Congress, the
largest library in the world, and discusses its current collections
and challenges.
   ISBN: 0-516-20940-X (lib.bdg.)   0-516-26395-1 (pbk.)
   1. Library of Congress—Juvenile literature. 2. National
libraries—Washington (D.C.)—Juvenile literature. [1. Library of
Congress. 2. Libraries.] I. Title. II. Series.
Z733.U58S17   1998
027.573—dc21
                                             97-29722
                                                CIP
                                                 AC

More than two thousand years ago, the royal library in Alexandria, Egypt, was the greatest library on Earth. It held more than 500,000 papyrus scrolls that contained all the knowledge of the ancient world. The Alexandrian library thrived for six hundred years, but over the centuries its magnificent collections were destroyed by time, fire, and war. Now no trace of it remains.

Today, the United States Library of Congress is the world's largest library. It contains more than 100 million items, including 29 million books and pamphlets, 53 million manuscripts, and 4 million maps and atlases. In addition, the library has 15 million prints and photographs, 3.5 million musical works, 6 million microfilms, 2.3 million sound recordings, and 500,000 films. These

The Library of Congress is made up of three separate buildings.

research materials, in more than 460 languages, are stored on 532 miles (856 kilometers) of shelving in three buildings in Washington, D.C. The library adds about one million new items to its permanent collections each year.

James Madison is credited with the idea for a library for the members of Congress.

The Library of Congress began as a small collection of reference books for the United States Congress. Members of Congress were educated men who often read books on history, philosophy, and other subjects for information to help them make laws and run the country wisely. In 1783, James Madison, who later became the fourth president of the United States, suggested establishing a congressional library. But Congress already had free access to well-stocked libraries while it met in the large cities of New York and Philadelphia.

Then, in the spring of 1800, the federal government moved from Philadelphia to the new capital of Washington, D.C. Washington was still a small village on the muddy banks of the Potomac River. There were no libraries for miles. The need for a congressional library was obvious.

Congress passed a bill setting aside $5,000 "for the purchase of such books as may be necessary for the use of Congress at the said city of Washington, and for fitting up a suitable apartment for containing them." President John Adams approved the bill

Washington, D.C., in 1800, before it became the nation's capital

Construction of the U.S. Capitol began in 1793. It was not completed until 1863.

on April 24, 1800. This date marks the official founding of the Library of Congress.

Congress placed a large order with the London booksellers Cadell and Davies, and a handsome room in the still uncompleted Capitol building was furnished for the library's use. Early in 1801, eleven trunks containing 740 books and three maps in a special case arrived aboard the ship *American*.

A Joint Committee on the Library of Congress, composed of three members from the House of Representatives and three members from the Senate, controlled the library's funds and made the major decisions concerning how the library would function. Members of Congress, the president, and the vice president were allowed to borrow books from the library.

John Adams served as the second president of the United States from 1797 to 1801.

Thomas Jefferson, third president of the United States

President Thomas Jefferson (1801–09) took a personal interest in the new Library of Congress. Jefferson was a noted scholar with a broad range of interests. His own private library included thousands of books on law, government, history, philosophy, science, literature, and the arts. The committee asked Jefferson to prepare a list of recommended books to include in the Library of Congress.

In 1802, President Jefferson appointed John James Beckley as the first librarian of Congress. Beckley was a political ally of Jefferson's who also served as the clerk of the House of Representatives. Congress voted to pay Beckley two dollars "for every day of necessary attendance" at the library.

Beckley encouraged authors and publishers of new American books to donate copies of their works to the Library of Congress. He promised to display their books prominently in the library and to list them in future printed catalogs of the library's holdings. By 1814, through purchases and donations, the Library of Congress collection had grown to three thousand books.

The United States had been at war with Great Britain for two years when British forces invaded Washington, D.C., and set fire to the Capitol on August 24, 1814. The Library of Congress went up in flames, and most of the books were destroyed. Legend says that the British used the books as kindling to start the fire.

The war between the United States and Great Britain that resulted in the burning of the capital is known as the War of 1812.

By that time, Thomas Jefferson had retired from the presidency and was living at Monticello, his home in Virginia. He offered to sell his personal book collection to the Library of Congress as a way to quickly replace the library's losses. Jefferson's collection was the finest and largest personal library in the country at that time. He estimated his books at "between nine and ten thousand volumes" and said that they contained information "chiefly valuable in science and literature." Jefferson wrote about his library, "I do not know that it contains any branch of science which Congress would wish to exclude from their collection; there is, in fact, no subject to which a Member of Congress may not have occasion to refer."

This bust of Jefferson in the present Library of Congress is a reminder that Jefferson's personal library made up a vast portion of the library's collection.

A congressman does research in the Library of Congress.

An appraisal of Thomas Jefferson's library determined that there were 6,487 books in the collection, and they were valued at $23,950. Some members of Congress complained that the price was too high, the collection was too large and general, and there were too many books in foreign languages. Nevertheless, Congress agreed to pay Jefferson his full asking price.

Early in 1815, ten horse-drawn wagons delivered Thomas Jefferson's books to Blodget's Hotel on E Street in Washington. Blodget's Hotel was the only public building that escaped burning during the British invasion. As a result, Congress was meeting there until the Capitol was rebuilt.

Along with Thomas Jefferson's books, the Library of Congress adopted Jefferson's personal

system of book classification, or the organizing of books according to their characteristics. The books were organized into three main subject areas: memory, reason, and imagination. Although this system was confusing to most readers, the library continued to use it until the early 1900s.

Jefferson's collection had twice as many books as the

As the library grew in size and importance, it became known as a library for everyone in the United States.

library had lost in the fire, and they were more varied in subject. The size and broad range of Jefferson's collection changed the Library of Congress from a small library of specific subjects for congressmen. People were beginning to think of the Library of Congress as a national library.

By 1816, the attorney general, members of the Supreme Court, and members of the diplomatic corps (experts in dealing with foreign countries) were allowed to use the library. The librarian's salary was increased to $1,000 a year, and a full-time assistant for the librarian was hired at $800 a year. George Watterson, the third librarian of Congress, continued the practice of encouraging authors and publishers to donate copies of their works. Watterson promoted recognition of the Library of Congress as a national library, and he even called it "the Library of the United States." He ensured that the library would be both an information source for Congress and a library for the nation.

In 1818, the library finally moved from Blodget's Hotel to temporary quarters in the attic of the Capitol, which was still undergoing restoration. The library remained in the crowded attic rooms until 1824, when it moved downstairs to a newly finished Library Hall in the center of the building. The Library Hall was considered the most beautiful room in the entire city of Washington. The library became a popular site for visitors and a source of national pride.

In 1832, Congress established a two-thousand-volume Law Library as a department of the Library of Congress. The Law Library was housed in its own room near the Supreme Court's chambers in the Capitol.

The Library of Congress continued to grow, and by 1836, it had 24,000 books. The library began exchanging duplicate copies of books with other countries, and by 1850, it owned 55,000 books. Experts judged it to be a collection of great value. Then, disaster struck.

On December 24, 1851, fire broke out in the library. The Library of Congress lost nearly 35,000 books, including two-thirds of Thomas Jefferson's collection. The separate Law Library, which had grown to 20,000 volumes, escaped damage.

The Library Hall was repaired and fireproofed. From that time on, it was called the Iron Room because its ceilings, floors, bookshelves, and

furniture were all made of fireproof iron. The library repaired some damaged books and purchased many new ones. The summer after the fire the Library of Congress reopened with 25,000 books.

The Law Library contained a wealth of information in its two thousand books.

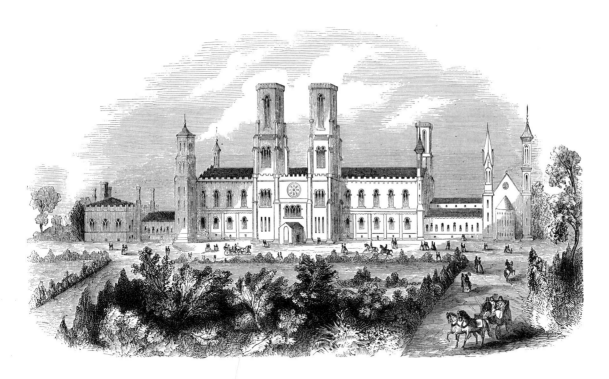

On December 31, 1864, President Abraham Lincoln (1860–65) appointed Ainsworth Rand Spofford as librarian of Congress. Spofford was determined to acquire as many books as possible. He wanted the library to contain "oceans of books and rivers of information."

When Spofford became librarian, the library had more than 80,000 books. The following year, Spofford acquired a donation of 40,000 books from the Smithsonian Institution. In exchange, Spofford promised the Smithsonian that the general public would be allowed to use the Library of Congress. Librarian Spofford also managed to purchase several important private book collections. By the end of 1869, the Library of Congress owned 237,000 volumes.

Then, in 1870, at the urging of Ainsworth Rand Spofford, Congress rewrote the copyright law. A copyright is the right to produce, publish, or sell a song, book, or other material. The copyright law protects artists and authors against the theft of their creations. No one may reproduce or perform a copyrighted work without the copyright holder's permission. Under the new law, the Copyright Office, which was responsible for registering all U.S. copyrights, became a department of the Library of Congress. As a result, the Library of Congress received two free copies of every item submitted for copyright registration in the United States.

This photo (taken in the late 1800s) shows books piled in almost any available space in the Capitol.

Librarian Spofford had been so successful at acquiring books that the library quickly ran out of storage space. In his annual report to Congress in 1872, Spofford wrote: "Masses of books, pamphlets, newspapers, [and] engravings . . . are necessarily always under the eye and almost under the feet of members of Congress and other visitors." In 1876, Spofford claimed that "books are now, from sheer force of necessity, being piled upon the floor in all directions."

Spofford finally convinced Congress that the library needed its own separate building, designed especially for library purposes. In 1886, Congress agreed to spend $500,000 to start construction of a new library building located east of the Capitol.

The massive, three-story building of gray New Hampshire granite covered an entire city block. It was designed in the architectural style of an age of learning called the Italian Renaissance (1350–1600). This ornate stone monument to human knowledge was intended to demonstrate the United States's great love of learning and to gain the respect and admiration of the world.

It took eleven years to complete the new building for the Library of Congress.

A fountain called "The Court of Neptune" rested in front of the main entrance. A bronze statue of Neptune, the ancient Roman god of the sea, was surrounded by sea horses and water nymphs. Massive, bronze entrance doors 14 feet (4 meters) high led to the spectacular Great Hall, which was filled with detailed artwork and ornamentation, including paintings, sculptures, murals, mosaics, marble columns, and stained glass. The interior of the magnificent building was constructed of the finest materials and elaborately decorated by the most skilled American artists and craftsmen.

The Great Hall is decorated with tall columns and spectacular artwork.

The newly constructed eight-sided Main Reading Room

The Great Hall led to the famous octagonal, or eight-sided, Main Reading Room. Circular desks provided enough space for 244 readers. The spacious chamber was crowned by a massive dome soaring 160 feet (49 m) into the air. A gilded Torch of Learning, to symbolize the library's purpose, topped the outside of the dome.

Construction of the new Library of Congress building was completed in 1897, at a total cost of $6,344,585.34. For three months during that summer and fall, workers transferred the library's materials to the new building by horse-drawn wagon. They moved 200,000 pamphlets, 18,000 volumes of newspapers and magazines, 200,000 musical scores and songs, 250,000 engravings, etchings, and photographs, and more than 40,000 maps and charts. Shelf-by-shelf, more than 750,000 books were moved—with great care taken to keep them in proper order. The new building provided storage capacity for more than two million books.

When the new library building opened its doors to the public on November 1, 1897, it housed a reading room, an art gallery, a hall of maps, the Copyright Office, and the Law Library. In addition, there were separate departments for periodicals (journals or magazines), music, manuscripts, and cataloging (a list of everything in the library). There was also a section for those who were responsible for maintaining the building and the grounds. The librarian's salary was $5,000 a year, and the staff consisted of 108 people.

In this 1897 photograph, visitors admire the architecture of the completed library.

The library's card catalog division, about 1915

There could no longer be any doubt that the Library of Congress was a true national library, containing a complete record of the history and accomplishments of the United States and the recorded achievements of all mankind. President William McKinley (1896–1901) called it "the national treasure-house of knowledge."

In April 1899, Herbert Putnam became librarian of Congress. Putnam was the first professional librarian to hold the position. He had been the head librarian of the Minneapolis Public Library and the Boston Public Library. When Putnam took over, the Library of Congress was still using Thomas Jefferson's method of classifying books. Putnam created an entirely new cataloging system that was much more efficient and useful, especially for an enormous collection like the library's.

The Library of Congress Classification system divided all knowledge into twenty major categories and assigned a set of letters and numbers to each subject area. It is still in widespread use today at the Library of Congress and other large research libraries. (Smaller libraries use the Dewey Decimal Classification system.) The Library of Congress reclassified its holdings according to

Surrounded by reference material, a member of the library's Congressional Research Service answers a call from a congressional assistant.

the new system and printed up catalog cards for all its materials.

Librarian Herbert Putnam was also responsible for a number of other innovations. For instance, he originated the interlibrary loan system of loaning books by mail to other libraries across the country. In 1915, Putnam created the Library of Congress Legislative Reference Service. The service was established to better fulfill the library's first responsibility of providing research and reference assistance to members of Congress. Renamed the Congressional Research Service in 1970, the department prepares reports on any topic at the request of a member of Congress. Today, Congress relies on the Congressional Research Service's staff of nine hundred specialists in fields such as law, economics, and the environment to provide unbiased information in response to 600,000 inquiries a year.

The Library of Congress had become the center of a national library system and "a bureau of information for the entire country," according to Librarian Putnam. By 1928, the library owned 3.5 million books and 10 million items total, and it employed 737 people. Not surprisingly, the library was again in desperate need of more room.

The library's space problems were solved temporarily with the opening of the five-story Annex Building in 1939. The Annex, located east of the Main Building and connected to it with a tunnel, provided shelf space for ten million books. The architecture of the white Georgia marble building was simple in style. The tall bronze entrance doors supplied an attractive accent, as did large murals in the two fifth-floor reading rooms.

When lack of space again became a problem, the Library of Congress James Madison Memorial Building was constructed south of the main library building. The plain, functional building of granite and marble has nine stories, three of them completely underground. It is the largest library building in the world. A large statue of James Madison, the fourth U.S. president, and the person who first suggested establishing a library for the use of Congress, is its main decorative feature.

The James Madison Memorial Building

When the Madison Building opened in 1980, the Annex building was renamed the Library of Congress John Adams Building. The main library building became the Library of Congress Thomas Jefferson Building. Together, the three Library of Congress buildings have about 71 acres (29 hectares) of floor space. The Jefferson Building has most of the public exhibition areas, while the Adams building is used primarily for storage (it holds two-thirds of all the library's books). The Madison Building is mainly offices, including the Congressional Research Service, the Copyright Office, the Manuscript Division, and the Law Library.

Today's Library of Congress is also a national cultural center and a living museum of American and world civilization. For example, the Library of Congress established the American Folklife Center in 1976 to preserve and promote American culture, including folklore, music, arts, and crafts. The American Folklife Center regularly sponsors special exhibits

An aerial view of the buildings of the Library of Congress

and outdoor folk music concerts. And in 1977, the Center for the Book was created to stimulate public interest in books and reading through a variety of programs, lectures, and exhibits.

The Library of Congress also benefits the public through the National Library Service for the Blind and Physically Handicapped. This service provides free loans of recorded and Braille books and magazines to people who cannot read standard printed materials.

In this 1933 photo, visitors to the library's Reading Room for the Blind take advantage of the library's Braille materials.

*Antonio Stradivari
made this cello
in 1697.*

*The everyday items
in Lincoln's
pockets the night
he died are now
priceless pieces of
U.S. history.*

The Library of Congress is not only the world's greatest source of information, it is also a storehouse of rare and valuable objects. The library owns three priceless violins, a viola, and a cello, all crafted by the famous 17th-century master violin maker, Antonio Stradivari.

The library holds the personal papers of most U.S. presidents from George Washington (1789–97) to Calvin Coolidge (1923–29), including Thomas Jefferson's original rough draft of the Declaration of Independence (1776). The document is in Jefferson's own handwriting, with scribbled changes by Benjamin Franklin and John Adams.

The library also owns the items President Abraham Lincoln had in his pockets the night he was shot (April 14, 1865). Among the items were two pairs of gold-rimmed spectacles, a pocket knife, a billfold containing a Confederate five-dollar bill, and nine newspaper clippings praising him for actions he had taken while in office.

The library's collection of early books (printed before 1501) is the largest in the Western

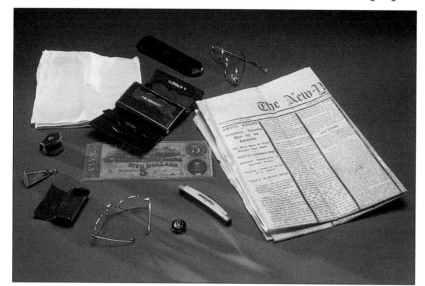

Hemisphere. The library also owns a copy of the Bay Psalm Book, the first book printed in what is now the United States. Published in Cambridge, Massachusetts, in 1640, it is one of eleven known copies in the world.

The library's Giant Bible of Mainz, a five-hundred-year-old illuminated manuscript Bible, is one of the last great hand-lettered books ever made. Its margins are decorated with beautifully painted birds, animals, and flowers. Johannes Gutenberg's invention of the printing press around 1450 effectively put an end to the creation of hand-lettered books.

The library also owns a perfect copy on vellum (high-quality parchment made from the skin of a calf, lamb, or baby goat) of the Gutenberg Bible. It is one of only three copies in existence. This Bible was the first book printed with a printing press and movable metal type. It is one of the world's most famous and valuable books. Both the Gutenberg Bible and the Giant Bible of Mainz are on permanent display in the Jefferson Building's Great Hall.

A page from the Gutenberg Bible shows the meticulous detail that Gutenberg put into his work.

One of the reading rooms available for visitors to engage in their research

Visitors to Washington, D.C., can take free guided tours of the Library of Congress. One million tourists, researchers, and scholars visit the library each year. Anyone above high school age who is engaged in serious research may use the library's collections. However, unlike local public libraries, the Library of Congress does not allow readers to browse through the stacks of books, and no one is allowed to take materials home. A researcher must fill out a call slip requesting a certain item and turn the slip in at the central desk. Then, librarians will locate the material and deliver it to the researcher, usually in less than an hour.

The same careful attention to the restoration of books is also given to the library's paintings and murals.

The Library of Congress faces many challenges as it enters the 21st century. Unfortunately, a large number of items in the library's collections are deteriorating due to age and environmental damage. In the case of rare or unique books, where the actual volume itself is valuable, experts must painstakingly restore each item by hand.

A technician photographs a book for storage on microfilm.

Numerous books, whose only value is the information they contain, are rotting away due to the acid content in their paper. The library has experimented with various methods of removing acid from paper. The library has also made an extensive effort to transfer valuable information to microfilm, a system that stores data by photographing each page. However, microfilm itself deteriorates after thirty or forty years.

The solution to the information storage problem now seems to be digital storage and laser disk technology. A thin, 12-inch (30-centimeter) disk can hold 10,000 to 20,000 pages of text. A library study estimated that a "foot of . . . disks standing side by side will thus store over 10,000 volumes and eliminate the need for nearly 1,000 feet of shelving."

Similar technology can be used to bring the library's resources to more users. The Library of Congress is taking an active role in helping to establish an international electronic library. The goal is to create a true "library without walls," where digital collections of primary research materials would be available to anyone who has the use of a computer and a modem.

As a first step, the Library of Congress completely computerized its cataloging functions in 1981. On December 31, 1980, the library added the last new card to its old-fashioned card catalog drawers. The card catalog still contains more than 20 million cards in 25,548 small file drawers. But the millions of new items added to the library's collection since January 2, 1981, can be found only in the computerized database.

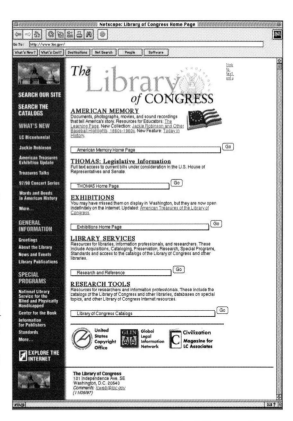

The Library of Congress website offers a chance to visit the library without traveling to Washington, D.C.

Computer users with access to the Internet computer network can visit the Library of Congress web page at *http://www.loc.gov.* In addition to the library's collection database, a number of interesting special exhibits and general information about the library are available on the web page.

Librarian of Congress James H. Billington declared, "By the library's bicentennial in the year 2000, . . . we aim to digitize millions of items and make them available on the Internet." Without a doubt, the Library of Congress will continue to take a leadership role "in helping turn information into knowledge."

GLOSSARY

annex – building added to a larger building

bicentennial – two hundredth birthday or anniversary

Braille – system of writing for the blind using characters made of raised dots on paper that people can read with their fingers

database – large collection of information, organized in a logical and useful manner, usually stored in a computer

gilded

gilded – coated with a thin layer of gold

illuminated manuscript – an original, handwritten document decorated with beautiful handpainted designs and pictures in colors (and sometimes in gold)

innovation – new idea or invention

modem – electronic device used to connect a computer to a telephone line

mosaic – picture made by setting small colored pieces of stone or tile into a surface

mosaic

mural – large painting applied directly to a wall or ceiling

nymph – in ancient Greek and Roman stories, a beautiful female spirit or goddess who lived in a forest, a meadow, a mountain, or a stream

ornate – richly decorated

papyrus – writing material made from the stems of the papyrus plant that grows along the Nile River in Egypt

scrolls – long strips of rolled papyrus, paper, or other writing material

TIMELINE

American Revolutionary War { **1775**
                              1781

Library of Congress established **1800**

1812 War of 1812 begins
1814 Library of Congress burned
1815

Fire destroys two-thirds **1851**
of library's holdings

Library of Congress
buys Jefferson's
collection; War of
1812 ends

1897 First Library of Congress
          building opens

1939 Library's Annex Building opens

1980
1981 Library switches to
          computerized catalog system

2000 Bicentennial of the Library
          of Congress

James Madison
Memorial
Building opens

INDEX *(Boldface page numbers indicate illustrations.)*

PHOTO CREDITS

Photographs ©: Corbis-Bettmann: 5, 6, 22, 31 top left; Library of Congress: 2 (Michael Dersin), 3, 27, 30 top (Carol M. Highsmith), 24 top (Dane Penland), 1, 13, 14, 16, 17, 18, 19, 20, 23, 24 bottom, 26, 28, 29; Mae Scanlan: cover, 8 top, 15, 21, 31 bottom left; North Wind Picture Archives: 4, 7, 8 bottom, 9, 11, 12, 25, 30 bottom, 31 right.

ABOUT THE AUTHOR

Gail Sakurai is a children's author who specializes in retelling folk tales and writing nonfiction for young readers. She is a full member of the Society of Children's Book Writers and Illustrators. *The Library of Congress* is her eighth book.

Ms. Sakurai lives in Cincinnati, Ohio, with her husband and two sons. When she is not researching or writing, she enjoys traveling with her family and visiting America's historical sites.